If I Have Seen

If I Have Seen

First edition: July, 2022

Layout and Design: Daniel Worley
Cover painting: Carolyn Wing Greenlee
Back cover photo: Daniel Worley

ISBN
978-1-887400-67-1 (paperback)
978-1-887400-68-8 (kindle)

Earthen Vessel Productions
www.earthen.com

Contents

INTRODUCTION

Poetry is personal. Some people like hearing what was on the author's mind, and some just want to experience the piece for themselves. For those who like to hear the story behind the poem, or are interested in some of the structural features I used to convey the message, or have trouble understanding poetry and would like some help comprehending words in that form, I've included explanations and background information.

For those who want to be left alone with the poem, skip the prose.

A word about senescence. It has to do with any kind of aging. I am now seventy-five. The society which worships youth and beauty declares I am officially antique and very nearly obsolete. There are physical, cultural, emotional issues lurking in that mellifluous word, senescence.

What does it take to grow deep at the root? Withstand separation and loss without losing hope? Have enough internal strength to keep growing towards the light when the way seems barred by impenetrable obstacles? How do we develop the character which, at the end of our lives, shows us to be more vibrant than in all our green years? And, in view of the terrifying specter of the Future Unknown, can God really turn it all to Good? These are questions I ponder as I continue to grow in this inevitable, ineffable senescence.

If you read the poems in order, you will get a sense of the rhythms of my life as I have come to appreciate my heritage, processed my losses, and discovered the treasures of darkness and hidden riches of secret places.

Carolyn Wing Greenlee
Lake County Poet Laureate #3 (2004-2006)

for Hedy
We took each other where we could not have gone alone

I Remember When Poetry First Rolled Over My Soul

I had never been
in so many minds
not mine
yet finding my Self
inside
without having
to knock
I was surprised
drowned by
sound
rolling over my soul
as if I were a whisper
and only It
was real

LALU

They called her "Poly" because the men at the mining camp couldn't pronounce "Lalu." Her father called her "Thousand Pieces of Gold," though I doubt he got that much when he sold her during the famine of 1871. She was taken to Idaho to be "Hundred men's wife." But she wasn't having it. A spunky gal, she managed not to serve, and, astonishingly, a kindly man named Charlie Bemis won her in a poker game and took her to be his wife.

Polly Bemis was a real person. An oral history of her was collected by Sister Alfreda, a nun in Cottonwood, and the accounts of the little Chinese woman who became respected and appreciated by the miners there became an historical novel by Ruthann Lum Macunn and then a movie.

I saw "Thousand Pieces of Gold," the movie, when I was forty-five years old upon the recommendation of a friend who told me it made her think of me, since my father's mother had also been sold during a famine and brought to San Francisco to serve as a maid in a wealthy Chinese woman's "house," though she was only four. I had just learned of her from my father as I struggled to make peace with my heritage. I really didn't want to be Chinese. I wanted to be like everyone else, judged, not on my face, but on who I was as a person.

I was born in the 1940s and had never felt visible. Growing up, the only people I ever saw in movies or TV who looked like me were shuffling cooks or ragged, coolies speaking ridiculous broken English. Heroines were curvy, busty, blue-eyed, pale-haired, and gorgeous. I wasn't anything like that.

And then I saw the movie, watching mesmerized till the last scene when Polly pauses upon a big horse, her black hair caught by the wind, beautiful, dignified, and completely whole. I rushed over to the table and began writing furiously. In ten minutes, I had this poem. And something more. I had seen an admirable Chinese woman, a real one, and I loved her. That began my efforts to collect and write the inside view of Chinese

American life as seen by five generations of my family. There was a sixth, my mother's father's father, but he came in 1874 and left many years later, one of the few who was able to return home. My mother's father came in 1899, a paper child pretending to be the 18-year-old son of San Francisco residents. He was only 14. When he was grown, he returned to Gong Village where he married his picture bride. My mother had five siblings, and not one of them spoke broken English. Mother loved reading Shakespeare. Uncle Walter taught physics at San Jose State and did research with William Shockley, who had won the Nobel Prize for co-inventing transistors.

I've spent the last thirty years telling our stories in memoirs and in poetry, and I have not only made peace with my lineage, I joyfully accept and embrace it as a true gift from God. But it began with Polly's story, which inspired me to tell my own.

Years later, I made a pilgrimage to Cottonwood, Idaho, to the small museum near the convent where Sister Alfreda lived. I saw the tiny intricate golden sculptures Poly had made from nuggets the miners had given to her to transform into works of art. I was so inspired by Lalu's life, transformed by her choices and the choices of those around her. It inspires me still.

Every life is a story, my mother used to say. Yes, unique and precious. I have spent nearly half my life collecting and telling as many true stories as I could, including my mother's growing up inside her parents' laundry, and my father's as a scrappy, barefooted farm boy. Together, they changed the world, literally, with what they pioneered. I've written those stories too. Story is important. It's how we see the effects of choices—where we go, what we do and don't do. It makes available to others the details of a life they could never otherwise know. And who knows what good may come from somebody reading their story? or mine? or yours?

By the way, my Chinese name is Lin Fa. If you can't pronounce it, you may call me Carolyn.

FROM LIN FA TO LALU
or From Carolyn to Polly
or To Thousand Pieces Of Gold from a buck ninety-five

Thick shine
long sweep
Chinese hair
black as ink sticks
rubbed fine on stone
watered
light reflecting whiter
against the rich dark

Her eyes
clear
do not appear
slanted
(the embarrassing adjective shaming me)
My soul
leaps to hers
grieves her fears
chafes her captivity
groans her indignities
entwines tightly with her
good brain
her
fine heart

Forty-five years
of other faces
other hair
curly
bright
blonde
red
freckled
blue
fluffy
flashy
laughing

curved-calved
heavy-breasted
full-hipped
swaying on stiletto heels

I—
clumping in oxfords
thin sticks terminating in Clydesdale hooves
dark
plain
disciplined
straight-backed Oriental ways
hard
as carved teak chairs

Then she
(who could have been my father's mother)
drew me as a little child
called me to live free
in a wild white place
I embraced her
kissed her
embraced and kissed myself
braided my hair like hers,
tying the ends in red for happiness

Thick shine
long sweep
Chinese hair
black as ink sticks
rubbed fine on stone
The wind laughs
tossing my hair
black brush strokes
on wide
white
sky.

WE WOLVES

My younger son Thomas was home from college on Christmas break. I was brushing my teeth when he surprised me by walking into my bathroom to talk to me. I thought bathroom time was private, but there he was, as if it were the most natural thing to talk to his mom whenever he wanted, wherever I was.

Life is dangerous these days, and the world outside my doors is full of hazards, but there are some who will always have full access to me, those I actually want to come close and receive all I can give them, my pups whom I love and from whom I have no need to protect myself.

We Wolves is centered, because my mom-heart is centered on my pups.

One of my favorite features of this poem is the deliberately ambiguous placement of some lines. Without punctuation to let you know what I intended the meaning to be, they can be read: "We wolves slouch low, don't show soft underbelly to nobody but pups." Or you can read it: We wolves slouch low, don't show soft underbelly to nobody. But pups are permitted..."

Poetry is a literary genre in which everything means something, including the placement, punctuation, capitalization (or lack thereof). I use my line breaks to help the reader experience the poem in the cadence I chose, because I use pauses and connections to make more clear what I'm trying to say.

WE WOLVES
for my sons

We Wolves
slouch low
don't show
soft underbelly
to nobody
but pups
are permitted
invited
desired
to drain
the surge
of milk
and love

STONES FOR BREAD

Before Jesus began His ministry on Earth, He went into the wilderness of Judea. In that desolate place, He fasted forty days and nights and prayed. After forty days without food, Scripture says, "He hungered." You think?

Right then, when Jesus was at the limits of His human strength, the devil showed up with three temptations. The first was pretty basic. "If you are the Son of God, command these stones to become bread." In other words, if you're really who you say you are, prove it. Meet your crying human need by doing a little miracle. No big deal. These stones look kind of like unleavened bread already, don't they? Just a little molecular rearrangement. Should be easy for you, right? Just say the word.

Jesus said, "It is written: Man does not live by bread alone, but by every word that comes out of the mouth of God." In other words, there is something much more life-sustaining than this material world. Yes, we need food, but we are more than physical beings. We have spirit and soul, and they require spiritual food.

Eve believed the lie that she could take things for herself outside of the will of God and it wouldn't make her die. But it always does, though not immediately. It's a slow dessication that ends in dust. It never satisfies.

When the children of Israel complained in the desert that they wanted meat, not this abominable manna every day, God brought them quail, but while it was still between their teeth, it gave them leannesss of soul.

Human hunger is deeper than bread; it's a craving for the Divine, the fulfillment that comes only when lived in close communion with the One Who designed each one with purpose only He knows and can reveal.

On the other hand, the miraculous is all around us—lessons from Earth. Seeds sprout and grow and make more seeds—grain to harvest we can make into bread. How does that happen? It's the life God embedded inside each seed—something invisible and irresistible, indomitable, ineffable. But it takes time. Can we wait for God's perfect orchestration of provision for our lives?

We have needs—crying human needs. We have to have water. We have to have food. And we have to have hope that does not disappoint. Time and again, God provides, even if it means manifesting manna, the bread of heaven, every day (except Sabbath) for forty years, and splitting a forty-foot high rock to pour forth good, sweet water in abundance for more than 2,000,000 people and animals for nearly two years.

But what about me? There are times all I see is hard red rocks—no water, no food, no shade. I have real,, verifiable human needs and no way to meet them. Am I really facing this wilderness journey alone? It's not a question of God's power and capabilities; it's about His character. Does He care, or are we, as so many believe, merely another species of beast crawling around on the face of the earth with no purpose or meaning beyond survival and what we can create for ourselves?

Jesus said, "Which of you, if his son asks for bread, will give him a stone? ...If you know how to give good gifts to your children, how much more will your Father Who is in heaven give good things to those who ask Him!" So I talk to Him, my Heavenly Father, and He sustains me, I don't know how. Miraculously, seeds sprout, pushing with all their might through the sun-baked earth, and what seemed hard as stone yields truth of His loving guidance that transforms the most difficult into good I can count on. He pours out living water that refreshes my bewildered heart when I feel most withered. Confusion and chaos fade into peace. He gives me food to eat, water to drink, His nurturing presence, and flowers to feed my soul.

WOULD YOUR FATHER GIVE YOU STONES FOR BREAD?

Even if I *could* turn stones to bread
would bites be delightful
or by the second mouthful
turn from grain to gravel
crushed to powder
dust of heights
ground down
Heaven's Wisdom Way
disrupted
disarrayed
dismayed
and stopped
by my own clay

The shoot slides up
then the stalk
then the head.
We don't know how it happens
but it does.
The life is in the grain of wheat
that falls to earth and dies.
The patient farmer waits
and is first to partake.

In Time,
You make all beautiful.
In Time,
You make Stone edible.
In the hopeless dust of wilderness,
You are our supply.
Great Stone Rejected by Builders,
You are our surprise:
Priceless Bread of Heaven
Precious Bread of Life

LORD,
I wait
and YOU talk
Manna from Heaven
Water from Rock

STAYING

I divorced my first husband because he no longer made my heart go pitter-pat. From everything I saw and heard—songs to movies and books, and societal values and beliefs around me—those are legitimate grounds to leave. We had grown apart.

But marriage is not so your spouse can make you happy. Or so you can complete each other. If you're not both whole people when you get married, you'll try to make each other fill in the gaps that are there in your heart. It doesn't work.

But there is something about keeping your vows, of choosing to stay anyway, of not making it all about yourself. Nothing challenges self-centeredness as much as marriage, and nothing has such potential to build tensile strength and depth and character as much as taking seriously what you vowed before God and people—for richer or poorer, in sickness and in health, for better or worse, till death. I'm not saying we should continue in a violent, abusive, unfaithful relationship. I'm saying people give up too easily. And God can do wonders if we let Him, but for that to happen, you have to stay.

STAYING

The old covenant
is worth the sweat
isn't it?
Vows are meant
to be kept
not fractured
just because
we're tired
irritated
sore
bored

Depths in your soul
are possible
when you choose to choose
what you chose before
for better
or worse
even when worse
goes on
and on
and on

Honor is rare
Effort
the surprise
that rises
from the heart
that continues
to try

Love roots down
long
well-branched
firm-grounded
because
flowers
are not the only good reason
to stay.

Prayer Flowers

Jesus,
When the enemy is firing
And the fiery darts are flying,
I don't need a friend with flowers,
I need a friend with faith
Who can help me see my Savior
Through the smoke and strange behavior.
Through the lies that boast and tower,
I need a friend who prays.

I need a friend who'll praise,
Who'll remind me of Your power
To keep, secure, and save
Till my understanding flowers
With the wisdom of Your ways.

SPARROWS

little birds
brown and plain
are not less noticed
than flashing stallions
sea-churning whales
or cool, still herons
blue on blue

little birds
fly into windows
lie broken on the roof
while wild winter rains
scour their feathers
from the glass
and nearly nobody knows
or cares

a billion people elsewhere
could care less
about our tears, our deaths
but Jesus sees the brown and plain
broken against the window pane
and recalls the hot sun
and the grit
of Jerusalem
dirt

LIGHT WORKS

earth's sweet fire
is but a moth
battering dust against the wide pane of Eternity
Beyond,
His Voice
makes the fragrant colors dance
and the Song goes on
Forever

JOY LUCK

I try to make my poetry say rather obviously what I mean. I used the sounds of the words, the phrasing, the arrangement on the page, punctuation (or lack thereof), to provide clear signposts so, at the end, you have experienced inside your being the meaning I intended you to have.

But this poem isn't like that. It requires work. So I'll help you out.

There are three sections. The first is a musing after I watched the movie, "Joy Luck Club." Interestingly, my parents weren't impressed. They left the theater with a disappointed feel about them. "Ho hum. Isn't that how it was with all of us?"

I knew my parents' pasts. The kind of horrors each of the mothers in the movie had suffered were not more remarkable than their own. Their parents had experienced even worse. But I, Third Generation Chinese American, had been shielded as best they could, and educated in a fine, ivy league university, and given every advantage they could arrange. And, like the girls in the movie, I didn't understand my parents' hardness and difficult ways.

Part 2: When I was shopping for a piano, the salesman showed me a Charles Walter upright. It had a beautiful voice and was very expensive. In order to help me understand the uniqueness of this hand-made piano, he explained that the sounding board was crafted from a very select kind of tree—Sitka spruce—and only those which have grown up on the windward side of the island where the lashing winds are the most severe. It forces their internal structure to be close-grained, which then has an extraordinary capability to transmit sound responsively, flavored with the depths of its cellular structures.

The third part is from Psalm 48:12-14 in the Amplified Version, which includes the overtones of the original languages. In this song, the sons of Korah tell their people to walk about and count up the towers representing noble deeds of past days, and think about ramparts, palaces, and citadels—all parts of a fortified castle. Why? So you can tell the next generation what they have received of internal strengths, glories, and resources that enable them to withstand the onslaughts that inevitably come in the process of human life. But there's more: "and cease recalling disappointments." Why? Because we are part of a continuing line of generations, each with its troubles, victories, and wisdoms—contributions to what has gone before. And through it all, we have this assurance—that this God is our God forever; He will be our guide, helping us find our way through what we've inherited and what towers, ramparts, palaces, and citadels we choose to build for our offspring till the end of all our days.

Now, here's the hard work. Juxtaposing these three sections, what do you get? I could tell you, but the wonder of poetry is it leaves room for you to get inside and find your own meaning in the context of your own history.

JOY LUCK

Is it the way of all mothers and daughters,
or uniquely Oriental,
the fussy small old lady
with irritatingly immovable ways?
Will I become one?
shrink & shrivel & snivel
or chatter drivel,
running out my words in trivialities?
I look like the girls in the movie—
sleek
advantaged
cat calm outside
cat scritchy inside
We are all taller than our mothers,
but they have grit from what they endured—
and because they sacrificed
to spare us from such things,
in some ways we will never grow as tall

On the windward side of the mountains
in the Aleutian Island chain
ripping winds assail Sitka spruce
which grow close-grained
prized as sounding boards
because they transmit most faithfully
whatever the Master plays.

Walk around Zion, and go round about her,
number her towers
(her lofty and noble deeds of past days),
consider well her ramparts,
go through her palaces and citadels,
that you may tell the next generation
[and cease recalling disappointments].
For this God is our God
forever and ever;
He will be our guide
even until death

Turgor Pressure

What makes it possible for a plant to push its way up through a hairline crack, widening the gap as it grows? Turgor pressure—the force of fluid against the cell membrane. When the cell is full of fluid, it makes the cell wall rigid. What happens when turgor pressure is low? Think limp carrot.

The cells in human beings also have turgor pressure. To me, it represents a wholeness of being that enables a person to bear up under pressure, press through obstacles, survive inhospitable environments, and retain integrity without compromising values or character.

People cannot pick their parents, their place in time or neighborhood, but they can flourish in the midst nonetheless.

In the first stanza of this poem, different difficult environments on the planet are cited, each one indicated with a capital letter followed by lines without punctuation or capitalization, their attributes elaborating on their forceful establishment. I used violent words: blasting, rampaging, forcing, followed by seemingly contradictory terms such as jaunty and fluttering. To me "dauntless Hello" belies the challenging nature of their placement on Earth. No matter how harsh, turgor pressure makes it possible for each life to flourish in the place it's planted, irrepressible, invincible, valiant, and whole.

TURGOR PRESSURE

Harsh calling
Sleek journey
Will we never flower full?
Tundra petals
blasting the ice night
jaunty in arctic white
Rampaging past
cracks tinier than
craze on a Chinese vase
Forcing into bonebaking day
their fleeting
fluttering
dauntless
Hello

Irrepressible Life
presses from
invincible Truth
valiant in crags and alleys
whole as summer afternoons

ANNA CHRISTINE

black hair
brown eyes
almond shape
no surprise

you look like her
you look like him
you are yourself
and both of them

who you are inside delicate skin
God only knows

but we will love
to help Him
help you out

3-23-95

I Like My Poetry

I like my poetry.
I am not like the eloquent Chinese boy
still wrestling to please his dead father
hating his poetry
feeling always it is not good enough.

I like the stretch of syllables in the spoken word—
the pressure of inflection, dips, and pauses.
Is it unseemly?

I like to read my own out loud,
playing with velvet and
the tips of consonants.
Should I be ashamed?

I am poethussy
shaking my syllables
flaunting my floribunda
flashing my
well-turned phrase

Should I be embarrassed
to be so pleased
with words
that close with the solid satisfaction
of a well-made carriage door?

WILDFLOWER SEASON

Whenever I look at wildflowers, I am impressed with their variety of colors, shapes, places, and times. Here in Lake County, California, some bloom in the shade and only in early spring, some appear abundantly during peak season, and some, remarkably, raise their yellow heads only late in summer in the driest and harshest heat. I am impressed by their opulent display flung lavishly by an extravagant Hand. And I am aware how quickly they die.

More and more I am coming to recognize how fleeting are the wonders of this life, but moments, like flowers, need not be lost. Memories hold them in the eyes. Poetry passes them along in bouquets we gather for ourselves. May we never overlook the small, or fail to appreciate the gift of time and the uniqueness of one another. It's wildflower season.

WILDFLOWER SEASON

We are wildflowers
scattered, wind-sown
warm, rich meadows are our homes
ice regions of the North
cracks of rocks
cheerful cascadings
celebrating roots that hold

We are often individually unseen
We have beauties known
mostly to ourselves
We have learned to live
where greenhouse flowers die
we, who are vapor ourselves

From the window of a passing car
we are massing, all alike
an array of force and color covering the world.
From where we sit, we are each ourselves
separate but close
opening and closing alone

We bring delight with variety
tears with the soft yellow dust of our fertility
we are opulent, lush, generous, gone
trusting the rest to integrity of seeds
and the faithfulness
of tomorrow

Watching the Super I Max feature, "Alaska," I was overwhelmed by the sight of salmon leaping vertically up a giant waterfall that seemed to be six stories high. How tiny they were!—how impossible their task! Battered to shreds, the fish finally reached their destination where they spawned and died. The scene changed to show eggs magnified so large they filled the screen. The narrator said they would develop and grow "in water enriched by their parents' decomposing bodies."

This poem is for my grandfather, his father, and all immigrants who came to the Land of the Golden Mountain seeking to give their children a better life.

IMMIGRANTS

Water
pounds
straight
down.
Home lies
straight up.
Against such
rush & crash
you fling yourself
past rocks
bears
exhaustion
flailing air
gasping
iridescence gone
no glory left
save one:
this I do
for my young

WITH ALL DUE RESPECT

Thoughts for Jay at 2 in the morning after he said,
"You define yourself by the past; I define myself by the future."

Jay was searching for identity, rejecting his Jewish heritage in favor of Zen and Eastern philosophies. At the time, I was finally making peace with mine, appreciating the unique perspectives that came along with being Chinese. We had some long, animated conversations.

When I was little, my father designed a book plate for me. On it was a Chinese proverb that said, "An earlier generation blazes a trail on which a later generation travels." I disliked it immediately. I wanted to make my own mark, not follow in the tracks of people who had already explored their new frontiers. However, as I interviewed my parents during the seven months I was living with them while my father recuperated from his cancer surgery gone awry, I heard my mother's stories about life in the Chinese laundry, my father's running barefoot through the chicken *shee,* and understood at last why they were the way they were. They were the children of immigrants who came, not for adventure, but for survival. Back home, they were eating the bark off the trees. Back home was a lineage of physicians, teachers, and scholars, but here they had to make a new way. Knowing their stories helped me recognize that everything I had was because of what I received as they sacrificed to give us a chance.

After one particularly lively discussion of several hours, I found myself wakeful in the night, my mind still carrying on the conversation with Jay that had ended unresolved. This poem came from that.

WITH ALL DUE RESPECT

With All Due Respect, Sir,
We cannot redefine ourselves
except in disembodied mind.
Forever tales from former trails
remain firmly packed
from countless footsteps
of those who passed before.
Removing
from the continuum,
catapulting ahead
like cosmic time-space leap frog
powerfully disengaging from *chronos* time
is illusory.
We are bundled
in ineffable lines
invisible if you go alone ahead
haunting
as a single silk thread
insistent
as spider web.

Which means you can try to ignore your roots, but they're always
still there and as long as you deny them, they'll continue to pop
up and shock you in compulsive, and sometimes embarrassing
behaviors. They are waiting, hoping someday to be recognized,
not as bondage, but as belonging.

More than twenty years ago, James BlueWolf (Lake County Poet Laureate #2) invited me to join him and Jim Lyle (Lake County Poet Laureate #1) doing public readings in round-robin-style. We were, as we described ourselves, a Dust Bowl Okie, a mixed-blood Chocktaw, and a Third Generation Chinese American. Dan Worley called us "Poetrio," and the name stuck.

Dan and I loved the poetry that James and Jim wrote, and decided to publish their work through Earthen Vessel Productions. I helped both poets prepare their work for publication, going through each poem on paper to correct punctuation and structure. Both were superb readers, and we soon discovered that they had been "cheating," speaking the words so the cadences fell out pleasingly. But when confronted with silent bare words on a page, the weaknesses showed up. And neither of these superb wordsmiths could punctuate worth a darn.

I spent hours going over James' poetry, making sure the words on the page reflected what he really meant to say. We also talked about our cultures, which were astonishingly different, almost opposite in some ways. For example, the Chinese believed everything had to be written down so it would be preserved accurately and could not be misunderstood. But in "Indin" culture (he said that's what they call themselves), things are passed down by words spoken to prepared and worthy ears. Only then could they be transmitted accurately and not be misunderstood. When James and I talked about this, we agreed that both approaches are valid, reasonable, right and true.

I call this poem "Editing in Three Worlds," because James is from one world, I am from another, and we are both from the one in which we live. Being mixed, he has struggled all his life to find the place he truly belongs. He said the Skins don't respect him as a real Indin. His blue eyes prove he isn't pure like them. And even though he has studied with the Elders and knows the language (which many Skins don't), they still look down on him.

I am pure Chinese, but my parents didn't teach me *Sam Yup*, our difficult dialect, wanting me to assimilate instead. Most of my life I struggled to belong—being too "other" for most of the folks, and being "a banana" to some of the more militant of my own race (yellow on the outside, white on the inside).

What Poetrio found, as we read our poems one after another, was how very much we loved and valued the same things. We wrote about people who had influenced us. We wrote about foods, joys, loves, loss, relationships, aging, death, hope. And we saw how, in the deepest, most essential ways, we are fully and warmly and wonderfully the same.

EDITING IN THREE WORLDS
for James BlueWolf

We sit
side by side
you with blue eyes
struggling to retain
your Indin side
me, Third Generation Americanized
yet these chosen words
arrayed before us
like Long Life noodles in porcelain bowls
celebrate centuries
rivers
wisdoms
dance
beckon to the stranger
bid me enter
see how we differ
feel how we're the same
groping for place
tribe
song

I am proud of who I am
I am proud of who you are
In all hearts Eternity calls
beyond all other
belongings

It started with the trembling. Doctor said it was Parkinson's Plus. My dad didn't agree. He thought it was more like ALS, but he didn't tell her. Parkinsons' can go on many years, gradually taking more and more, but not a fast plummet from normal to wheelchair to death. One of his engineers had it. He was dead in just three years.

So I don't know what she actually had, but it shook all of us. She had always been steady, unshakable, but the prospect was grim and all of us felt the earthquake making it hard to keep our balance. Overwhelmed, I retreated into poetry and wrote a lot of it. Most of it wasn't very good.

In deciduous trees, the reds and yellows are always present in the leaf, but chlorophyll masks them until cold weather signals the plant to start gathering its energy back into itself. As the chlorophyll withdraws, the brilliant pigments are revealed.
Autumn leaf became an evocative image for my mother as I described the withering of hope, the osteoporosis that riddled her bones with holes that crushed and fractured as she fell. Birds have bones that are full of holes. It makes them light enough to fly. But, in her case, Mom's bones kept breaking, adding to her losses till she couldn't even get out of bed.

But she surprised us. She adjusted her sense of future. She continued to live and be transformed in ways that I never would have guessed. All her years, she'd had to fight for her life—as the unloved eldest daughter of her difficult mother, as an unloved race living in a hostile society, as the Confucian family slave— the wife of the youngest son. But she had guts. She had fought her way through every hard thing, and now, fighting for each day of breaths, she stunned me with her colors and her courage, gift of strength from pressing on through a life of adversity..

MOTHER AS AUTUMN LEAF

Sap retreats
leaves
wrinkle
drybrittle
bones afraid to fall
riddled with holes
birdlight
and shrinking

She is shaken
but in her shaking
more appears—
flexible
unabashed
sturdy
in beauty
and holding on—

Surprised
I recognize
all the years
under green
she's been living
gold vermillion.
She learned it
in the drought.

CHANGE OF FUTURE

When days thin to basics,
the future no longer stretches out
a seductive song
enticing and inviting—
it drags by
stripping
as we once pulled plums
from summer branches.

I thought I was a grown-up. I was in my fifties. If you're not a grown-up by then, when will you ever be?

Yet, there was that time... Daddy had gone to the store, leaving me to take care of Mom. I knew how. I'd even become rather good at suctioning her when she began to drown. I wasn't worried. We'd done this before.

But it was getting dark. I heard a siren in the distance. Daddy had been gone a long time. And suddenly I was that child again, kneeling on the couch, peering past the curtains of the window—as a matter of fact, it was this very window—and I felt as terrified as I had been many years of nights as I waited for my parents to get home.

Always Never Coming Home

Distant siren
fading day
say
They're never coming home.
I am twelve again.
I am nine.
So many nights
in front of the window
watching for headlights
listening for tires
as long as I remember
they were always
never coming home

I am fifty-one
mother of two
grandmother of three
president of a company
author of books
speaker before many
singer before crowds
I've traveled plenty
I have been a grown-up now
much longer
than I was a child

yet in the failing light
as distant sirens fade
I am twelve
I am nine
and they are never coming home

Bok Fahn

bok fahn—white rice
soong—everything else

You're supposed to eat a bite of *bok fahn* between each bite of *soong* so you can enjoy the full flavor of the dish without mixing it with other flavors.

BOK FAHN
In Honor of White Rice

Plain *bok fahn*,
fragrant steaming—
Taco Bell can't
set me dreaming.
Every kernel,
pure and sweet.
Lox and bagels
can't compete
with innocence
and soft demeanor.
Who'd prefer
a salty wiener?

Meek, supportive,
self-effacing,
willing so
to be the spacing.
Curry chicken,
broccoli beef—
too much flavor
needs relief.

Gentle *bok fahn*
clears the tongue,
setting, gemlike
every one of
sweet and bitter,
salty, sour.
Soong has praise,
but *bok fahn*, power.

I am intrigued by the Oregon/California Trail, fascinated with the people who made that journey, and why. I've studied it, read diaries and journals, published two—one of the first to make the trip, and one of the last.

My friend and hero, JoAnn Levy, wrote a book called *They Saw the Elephant*. She was dismayed that no women at all are mentioned in the most respected books on the gold rush. Were there no females who went West? Her research revealed many, and not all of them went reluctantly or hated it. Some made quite a good living sewing buttons, doing laundry, baking bread for miners who didn't want to take the time to do such things for themselves, preferring to have someone else do it, and they paid in gold.

In the 1990s, my husband Dennis and I made a trip from California to Missouri following the trail of Lewis and Clark, then returned via the Oregon/California Trail. It was a thrill to see Chimney Rock and to walk by Scotts Bluff, putting my feet in the deep wagon ruts that still remain, strong as stone.

There's a lot I could say about the images in this poem. Behind each one is profound acknowledgement of what those overlanders reported, but I want to tell you just two things.

First, I started writing this poem before we left on our trip, but I wasn't able to find an ending. Nothing rang true. But after several weeks in an ancient motorhome, experiencing the terrain and temperatures and adversities as we retraced that difficult journey, I came home and finished the poem. I had to live it before I could end it. I had to know inside myself what it really meant.

The other story is from the time I was reading my poetry at the California Arts Council's first gathering of all California poets laureate. Al Young, our state Poet Laureate was there, listening intently, encouraging us generously. I don't remember what I read, except I know this poem was one of them because, as I made my way back to my seat, Al leaned into the aisle and said to me, "When you read that poem, I really believed you were a Westward woman."

At that time, I was still reeling from my own change of terrain. Dennis had had one stroke, then another. I was still trying to care for him at home, wondering what to do and how to do it. On the long, arduous trail, Westward women had to adjust, adapt, invent, innovate, face their fears, leave their treasures by the road, bury their husbands, make their way alone to the end, the town they call Bend.

Now I too was truly a Westward woman finding my place in a new frontier.

WESTWARD WOMEN

Westward women
weren't always willing
but love
or fear
pressed them to beginning
from the spot called
"Independence"

Westward women
weren't the same when they arrived
as the ones they started out
as the ones they left behind

Westward women
buried husbands under trees
left their china in the dust
by castoff wheels
broken by ruts
by jostling and pounding
by parch
by scorch
by snow
drifted high and holy white
covering cattle
standing hollow
covering bellows
growing weaker
old and younger
growing weaker
hunger held them helpless
and boredom trudging step by step
counting dangers
two thousand miles

Westward Woman
figured out
how to fix a dandy meal
over buffalo dung
they selected themselves

no longer worried
about spoiling their hands
tried to describe
with words too small
what only Overlanders saw
spire stones
prairie dogs
yellow orange lace
under water smelling foul
prairies so flat
nothing stopped the wind
mountainsides so sheer
they broke your heart just to look

Westward Woman
made love
babies
home on the range
rinsed their dried red rags
discreetly
(when there was water)
kept their woman-hearts
discarded all the rest

When Westward women arrived
they had learned to improvise
set up new lives
in split skirts
riding astride
knew they were strong
could do a man's work and not be one
having driven cattle
battled bugs and varmints scuttling in darkness
and snakes

Westward women
couldn't wonder anymore
what folks back home would think—
they had become
Women of the West
and couldn't explain
or have to.

Most of the time when you see the symbol of the Tao, it's a circle with two raindrop shapes curving around each other, a drop of each in the center of the other. On paper, it looks black and white and flat, but my father told me it's actually like a baseball, with the *yang* and the *yin* wrapping around each other. The black part represents the *yin*. What you see as white is the *yang*, and it's actually red. In Taoism, everything is *yin* or *yang* in varying degrees *Yin* is cool, blue, ice, soft, receptive, dark, wet, female, internal, winter, deep. *Yang* is superficial, outsides, hard, dry, hot, summer, fire, penetrating, yellow, male. All males are *yang*, but not all *yang* is male. It's a principle, not a gender. And, as in everything, things can be varying degrees of *yang* or *yin*.

All that to say Dan Worley, my creative partner for over thirty years, is a very *yang* man. His hair is auburn, a shade of red. He is aggressive, impulsive, daring, adventuresome, rash, hasty, and sometimes alarming. Confucian-trained, I'm prudent, careful, hesitant, safety-minded, wary, and cautious. I like my ducks in a row. I don't want to make a move until I'm sure. Which is why God chose Dan to complete the team. God once told me, "If you wait until all your ducks are in a row you'll never do anything because your ducks will never all be in a row."

So God put Dan in my life to catapult me sometimes into places I would be afraid to go, but He also put me in Dan's life to be the brakes, the tether, the string that both constrains the kite and also helps it soar.

The American West
has long attracted
encouraged
rewarded
prized
I can
I will
Nothing ventured, nothing gained
He who hesitates is lost
No holds barred
Full speed ahead
all *yang*
no *yin*
which is where I
come in.
You say
When in doubt,
floor it.
I say
Look before you leap.
He sins who hastens with his feet.

You are red-haired. I have black.
I whisper caution. You attack.
In terms of partners, our balance is best:
My Great Wall crossing your American West.

For Grace Elizabeth

Dear Baby Grace
only 30 hours old,
when you are 30,
I'll be 82.
You shall think of me
as a very old granny indeed
and be amazed
that I know so many things.
It's from living long
you know.
You shall also know
much more than you do now
when you are as old
as I will be
when you are 30.
For now
before your little blank brain
is snapping arcs
leaping across space
with not much network branching
highways faster than a speeding bullet.
You know nothing of
autumn,
the splendid time
when all Earth changes to vibrant clothes
to celebrate
in honor
of
your birth.

11-17-99

ARTISAN FATHER

Where you are is
on the edge
boldly going
where no one else
would ever even think to go.
When you are ON,
you work your magic
and walls come tumbling down.
No one is stranger for long.
No one is safe from your charm.
Flashing, dancing,
you know how to make
the biggest splash
diving in
with both rash feet.
You heed no danger.
Accept no obstacle.
Enjoy the difficult
and often the impossible.

I admire
your derring-do,
dazzled by
your dashing heart.
If there's a risk,
you take it
never counting the cost—
leaving that
to Mom.

You can ignore us
run over us
insist,
resist—
unmovable
unreasonable
incomprehensible
crushingly implacable

You are infuriating
exasperating
frustrating
mystifying
magical
inaccessible—
you are definitely
inevitably
yourself.
No matter how irascible,
you've got your style.
Your life
is one continuous creative act
and even you
have no idea
where you're going,
nor do you care.
It's always new
adventure—
always
the perfect day
to go.

PAST HAUNTS

For years, I have prayed with people particularly for the healing of early childhood traumas. No matter how old we get, our past haunts us—unless we can release it into the hands of God, Who alone knows how to redeem each awful thing, no matter how terrible. He can transform it into a gift of comfort with which we can comfort others who have the same kinds of wounds.

Where I wanted the statement to feel open-ended, leaving room for more to follow, I did not close the thought with a period.

PAST HAUNTS

My history has holes
where whole should be
Who knows what happened
in the first 12 years?
Insubstantial,
I drifted into junior high
where I lodged in
incompletion to this day

They say
you can never heal those places
fill those spaces
I don't agree.
We can grieve
release
resolve
redeem
release
We can say
This wound does not define me
drive me
own me
We are flutes
not sticks.
We are lace that lets our faces touch
through the curtains of our pain

PAPER

paper—
thin
accepting
accommodating
easily torn
flexible
bland
blank
mute—
can turn a sudden edge
and slice you
red

December

September
We wonder
will she make 81?

November
she wants to see me
talk on the phone
I don't know what to say

December
She could make Christmas
anniversary 59

At year's end
with life counted in months
weeks days
how carefully I listen to the reedy voice
disappearing insufficient air

She knows me so strongly
long before memory
she has kept me
tells me
things I simply could not know
retrieves the deepest realities
if I care to ask
I pray
not to trespass
any closely-guarded ground

I listen
fearing fog will close her in
out of view
or hearing—
beyond her knowing
who I am,
who knew me from beginning
before I knew myself

22 months ago
she could
still run
sign her name
sit
eat
talk
slam doors
weep
loud enough to sound through the solid-core door
from the bed
where she'd flung herself
when she could still
fling

Reading words I wrote back then
immobilizing pain
I am shocked
at what's been lost
and gained
Wherever we place her now
she stays
sack of potatoes
looking up at us
She giggles
when she piddles on my wiping hand
passes gas when I pull her diaper up
helpless as a newborn
but not as loud
or selfish
Now she thanks my father
calls him her Sunshine
says he's the best
pleased that at last
she's first

My father says,
We'll go on as before.

Nothing's changed.
We're the same.
He's wrong. Nothing's the same.
Now she calls me her angel.
She never called me her angel.
I climb in beside her
daring to match
my grown-up frame to hers.
surprised to be so close
we've never been this close
I hold her like the cherished child
she never got to be
she sighs
closes her eyes
holds me like the cherished child
I never got to be

How Trees Survive

There's botany in this poem—the way trees react to the first frost. Leaves fall. All nonessentials must go so the tree can survive.

Between the first word and the question mark, there is deliberate ambiguity. It vacillates. You can read it a few different ways, depending on which lines you connect with the one before or after.

How do we react when circumstances strip us of our influence and presence, casting less than half our former shadow?

My mother knew how to dress with style—classic, yet daring. Daddy said the men at the Lions' Club used to say to their wives, "Why don't you dress like Kay?" But Mom never dressed to attract attention from men; she had been extremely poor, even in her early adult life, and, now that she could afford to, she dressed to entertain herself. And she was, very truly, quite gorgeous.

However, as the disease progressed, it was no longer practical to wear clothes that required dry cleaning. Jewels were a nuisance, and she could no longer balance in 3-inch heels—or any shoes at all.

I remember having to cut her Eddie Bauer sleeveless tee up the back so we could get it on and off her more easily. Clothes had been so important to her, and looking nice for Daddy. It brought tears to my eyes because I knew she would never again be the fabulous, flamboyant Kay Wing. But she never complained about that. She knew they were only externals.

In the next part of the poem, there is resolve. Each statement ends with a period. My mother was matter-of-fact. If it must be this way, then it must. In her life, she had endured many hard things. She knew how to adjust. Period.

Not that it wasn't difficult. She lost her ability to eat and swallow. Even water caused her to choke and feel like she was drowning.

She couldn't walk. Then her hands wouldn't work. She couldn't move her body. We had to turn her every two hours. And she could barely talk. Hard losses. They frightened her—and us. But she did not give up. She still wanted to live. I was told that, on the morning of the day she died, she was seen exercising the one arm that would still obey her.

The last part of the poem has no punctuation. It is meant to be read in one breath, as if hurrying to pull into itself all that remains of essentials.

There's something about knowing you will never get better, that this degeneration will continue taking your capabilities and your future until nothing is left. You have every day after long day, and even longer sleepless night, to contemplate your life— and death. It gives you time to decide what really matters, to make amends, to look back and see how far you've come.

In the end, my mother knew she had value, not because of what she could do or how she looked, but for who she was. It was no longer her performance, multi-tasking, running a multi-million dollar business, and keeping things together for everyone else, making sure all their needs were met. She couldn't do anything for anyone, and still we loved her. It healed her. It healed us. And she was not afraid to die.

How Trees Survive Winter

What I Learned from my Mother
Mother's Day, 2000

Do trees weep
lost leaves
when they stand stripped
casting less than
half the shadow
do they mourn
their former
glory?

Or when the first frost
snaps at their
proud array
do they say
Come quickly, Sap.
No regrets.
Abandon all vulnerabilities.
Concentrate
all green
centered
grow down
deeply
endure
in this
still safe place
await
the time
of blossoms

FAREWELL

I suppose it's a good sign
when you leave behind
a hole where you have been,
a place
no one can fill,
a space
your size
your shape
your depth

I suppose
if it closed
as wounds
scabbing over
fast and hard—
you could pass
to pleasant memory
and that would be that—

but it remains
a space
your size
your shape
your depth
a hole in my heart
that only you can fill,
an open place
that longs,
belongs
to you

How Long?

I learned about the Charles Bonnet Syndrome from the low vision specialist who was helping me adjust to the sudden loss of vision that came about, as does much vision loss, from unremitting stress over long periods of time. I had been taking care of my parents and husband, in varying degrees of emergency and chronic degenerative disease, for more than twenty years, and when my husband was finally settled in a care facility, I sat down to work at my computer and found I could no longer read.

Since 1984, I had known the cause of my night blindness was Retinitis Pigmentosa, a degenerative eye disease from a rare recessive gene that both of my parents carried. I knew my peripheral vision would diminish, like the f-stops of a camera lens, till the last pinpoint of light went black. Rods would continue to die, but I did not expect to lose the cones. It was shocking not to be able to distinguish between purple and brown, or recognize colors for the shades they really are. For some reason, that struck me with crushing grief. I had been a painter as well as a professional photographer. Somehow, the thought of not being able to see color was devastating.

According to the research of Charles Bonnet, people who have been sighted will continue to see vivid, detailed images even after all sight is gone. Some of the images are so realistic the person may think they're actually there—such as a building. In my case, I saw my cat.

It's as if the brain, deprived of its usual stimulation, wants to entertain itself. For a while, whenever I closed my eyes, I saw quilts in vibrant colors.

This poem is my reaction to that grief.

How Long?

Upon hearing of the Charles Bonnet Syndrome

It wasn't bad before
twenty
thirty
forty years
snapping pictures
catching light
gathering words
shelves of works I said I'd read someday

I don't remember when I stopped seeing stars

It's not all black
Sometimes it's gold
but mostly
it just
isn't

I see patterns now—
neon curls
comet swirls
They say my brain
wants to
entertain itself
making up
what it doesn't get
Last night I saw my cat
They say I'll see
visions
scenes
stored up vivid memories

Days go by
and every day
I feel I haven't done it right.
I haven't stopped to look or paint
or sorted everything I saved

Under mylar
all pictures feel the same

If I could keep this much
it wouldn't be so bad
Now every dusking
says
How long?
How long?
every night
declines into black
and
more black
a rehearsal
harbinger
decree

People lose much more than I
and still I whine.

Why can't I do this better?

How long
horsetail clouds
flicked white across high blue?
How long beloved faces
cavorting cat
movies
paintings
zoos
How long till cones and colors go
and all that is swift
shades to sound

Oh fill, eyes!
Fill and fill and fill
not with tears
no
with all that noiseless flies on silhouetted wings

I am alone
in this
unpredictable
patterned
made-up stuff
cats not there
and gold that does not make me rich
and colors I knew
are no longer true
f/8
f/16
f/22

How long?

GRATITUDE

I've heard that, of all the emotions, gratitude has the highest frequency. Higher than love. The emotion with the lowest frequency is self-pity. Interesting that one cancels the other, like noise-canceling headphones that play the reverse of the wave of the noise.

I wrote this poem while my mother was in the last stages of her degenerative neurological disease and my sight had tanked from the stress of caregiving her and my husband at opposite ends of the state. I was in perpetual toggle mode, always feeling I should be taking care of the other person 500 miles away.

It takes a lot of effort to be present, to feel the breeze and smell the morning. It requires deliberate intention to taste your food, and to chew it. A nutritionist at the Harvard School of Medicine said, if you multitask while eating (driving, talking on the phone, studying for an exam), you lose 30 to 40% of its absorption. God gave foods different scents, colors, shapes, textures, and flavors for a reason, and it wasn't just for nutritional value.

Life is meant to be savored, experienced, read with insight and understanding. If we rush along, watching traffic even if we're not the driver, we miss the landscape passing by. Deserts can look bland and boring mile after mile of the same, but if you stop and get down close the the hard-baked dirt, you might see tiny plants, belly flowers, so-named because you have to get down on your belly to see them. We miss so much as we drive past ("drive" being the operative word) because, at that speed, even masses of wildflowers look all alike, yellow or blue, and you never see how individually beautiful they are.

GRATITUDE

Be present.
Do not devour.
Savor flavors.
Feel flowers.
Notice the breeze
easy on the skin
gently lifting hair
bringing fragrance in

Chew.

Do not act as if
nothing smells
and everything tastes
the same

SEEING STARS

Not everything is loss, even as we grow older. Sometimes we get something back. Sometimes we see things in new ways, and they're brighter and more cherished than when we had everything in abundance and the future was still a long way off.

SEEING STARS

A Valentine from my Father

I saw stars last night.
They flickered in and out of the Nothing Place
like names on the tip of your tongue
like words you can almost remember
After years of not looking up
I was content to gaze at day
admiring clouds too big to miss

I have learned the paradox of loss
that treasures what's left
more than all I had before
final grains of rice
final whispered words
Every day I hope
to keep hold onto what I have
but I don't.
That's the way it goes:
with this
you never get anything back

But last night I forgot
I had stopped looking up
and there they were
bright & dim & many
flickering in and out of the Nothing Place
like names on the tip of your tongue
like words you can almost remember

Lunar Call

My father, who grew up on a couple of different farms in Central California, told me the Chinese workers would always do their planting according to the lunar calendar. He said the plants knew when to grow because they responded to the moon. Of course, how and when the moon speaks to the plants depends on where they are in relationship to each other. Summer in Australia is winter in California.

This poem is dedicated to my dear friend, Jim Lyle, who objected to one of my poems, saying I was not representing accurately the disenfranchised human population. I told him I was telling my story, not theirs, and that is a legitimate point of view. When I give talks on the Chinese American experience, and when I write about it, I'm not telling how it was to work in the mercury mines. My mother's parents owned a hand laundry. We cannot speak for all peoples, even if they come from the same country. We can only tell what we know, so I speak from my observations of how things are from my point of view, how it looks to me, at least, in my part of the world.

Lunar Call

for Jim Lyle

The moon rolls around
and the seeds go Yes!
the bulbs go Yes!
the trees go Yes!
The moon rolls around
and the earth says Yes!
at least
in my part of the world

The moon rolls around
and the seeds wake up
the trees wake up
the bulbs start to push
The moon rolls around
and the grass pricks up
at least
in my part of the world

The blossoms start
and the buds nub out
even if the winds lash the branches bare
"It's time" they say
"and we must obey
the stir
the urge
the Grow"

The Call comes deep
The Call comes soft
The Call comes strong
in the secret place
The Call comes sure
The Call comes true
The Call goes forth from the moon

And the seeds pop up
the blossoms roll

the green shows up
everywhere
and the flowers come
wild flowers come
at least
in my part of the world

DONNER POEM

Way back when I was teaching in the last century, I learned the term "situational ethics," with its premise that a decision to take a certain action is ethical depending on the circumstances. One of the exercises was called "The Lifeboat." You're in a lifeboat with limited resources. Also in the boat are, for example, an old lady, a child, and a drunk. You're asked to decide which one you would throw overboard first.

Many years later, I learned that this concept of flexible ethics comes from the idea that ethics are not based on any absolutes, but are the product of human thinking. According to this worldview, everything evolved from a single-cell ancestor, with all species resulting from eons of time with billions of chance mutations and random variations sorted out by natural selection. This explanation of the origins of life makes it unnecessary to believe in God. Without God to bring everything into being, there is no Mind, intention, no design, no purpose, no meaning, no accountability, no free will, no significance, no destiny, and nothing after death. We humans are free to create our own system of right and wrong based on what is right in our own eyes. It's helpful to know the entire title of the book that proposed this model that has so thoroughly affected our world today. It's *On the Origin of Species by Means of Natural Selection, or The Preservation of Favoured Races in the Struggle for Life.* As you can imagine, Hitler loved it.

I tell you this because I worried about the lifeboat and wondered who to throw over first. I was not a Christian, and I had no idea what was right or wrong based on a righteousness that came from the holy being of God. I worried that, under dire enough conditions, I would eat my friend. I was told, "You never know." But now that I've been a Christian for forty-five years, I do know. If I had to throw someone overboard, it would be me, and I'd tell the others I would be in heaven with the God I love. I would say I wanted them to live, and they too could know for sure that, when they died, heaven would be their home.

By the way, I studied the Donner party. It was gristly indeed, hearing horrifying quotes from diaries that said they fought for different body parts. But if there is no true God-ordained right and wrong, if survival of the fittest is our lot, then the only thing that matters is that you survive one more day. However, you still have to live with yourself afterwards, and how can you not remember?

Interestingly, the Reed family, including the children, all survived. One of the girls wrote that her family did not eat people, though they were the only ones who didn't. They survived on leather, and when they were rescued, there was still leather available. The Donner party did not have to eat each other to keep alive. One diary I read stated that they had chosen to eat people instead of leather. They were tired of leather.

We are surrounded by Survival of the Fittest, ethics decided based on circumstances. In business, politics, sports, relationships, and the world of academia, people devour one another as a matter of necessity, thinking nothing of it. But we don't have to. We can decide ahead of time what is true, good, and worth holding onto. It will keep us steady all the days of our lives. We are not recipients of fortuitous random mutations. We are unique creations, each one designed and loaded with good gifts from our Heavenly Father. We have free will and a chance to make the world a better place. This elegantly fine-tuned universe is the creation of Divine Design. The same God Who invented gravity and the orbits of planets ordained the laws—both physical and moral. When human beings align with God's ways, they have the most extraordinary fruitful and fulfilling lives. We are all going to die. How we handle it, and our present days, is our choice.

DONNER POEM

They say there's no way
you can know what you'll do
when snow piles high
and you can't get through.
But I'd rather fade
with my belly aquiver
than fight for a bite
of somebody's liver.

If I Have Seen

Charles Bonnet Syndrome

If I have seen
I can keep
this blue
lake under summer sky
lupine
collectively asserting their
upright buds
primly purpling over
drop-off cliffs
red dirt
violent under
sword blade grass
pale
new
promised
spring

If I have seen
this green
deeper than sleep
fragrant as morning
before dry noon
bleaches peach and lavender
to pristine egret white
I can keep dark detail
sketched in fractals
same
and not the same

Do not neglect
the blacks
the grays
thin fog
young dawn
subtle mottled
sea-smoothed stones
whispered shades

settling day
in silence

In my time
I have thrilled to
yellow dusted contoured hills
so common after miles
that I forget to say
oh look
oh look
oh soak
my eyes
in butter color
It doesn't last for long.

But even if I cease to see
I will know you
by your scent
by your sound
I will know you
by your song
And never see you fade.

PASSOVER

They would have eaten.
He would have broken
bread unleavened,
striped and pierced.
He would have given
the Cup of Redemption.
They would have sung
and after, gone out:

This is the day the Lord has made
I will rejoice and be glad in it

He would have led them
into a garden.
They would have slept.
He would have prayed.
He chose to be broken
like matzo unleavened
accepting the cup
of the Lamb of redemption.

He would be beaten
He would be hidden.
He would be brought out
Gift of Redemption.

Blood on the doorposts
Death passing over
matzo now broken
striped and pierced
Perfect Redemption
Death passing over
I will rejoice and be glad in it

Spring Happening With Hedy

Most people haven't a clue what it takes to be a guide dog team. I didn't. I'll tell you: It takes a lot of work. For a year (if you go by the book, and I do), you don't allow anyone else to interact with your guide—not to pet, feed, play, walk, talk, or even make eye contact. You have to be the source of everything to your guide, and she must not listen to any voice but yours. Why? Because your life depends on her, and even someone calling her name can distract her from paying attention to where you're going and you end up stepping in a hole and twisting your ankle or breaking your neck. Think of it as someone grabbing your steering wheel.

In a guide dog team, the bond is everything. It's what makes you sensitive to each other. It's what makes your guide want to keep you safe. Without the bond, you're left with a very expensive pet. Nobody can force a dog to guide. She has to want to.

When we met, Hedy and I did not immediately fall in love with each other. In fact, we rather disliked each other. In fact, I kept asking God if she really was His best choice for me, which is what I had been praying for the preceding year. I wasn't thrilled, but I had learned that, in every case, Father truly does know best, so I kept doing everything by the book and, to my amazement, after a while, it worked.

When the instructors asked me what I wanted in my guide dog, I left breed, gender, and color up to them, figuring they knew their dogs better than I, but I did request that she be smart and not obsequious. Hedy was not obsequious. She was aloof—at least, she was with me. She adored her trainer so much that he finally had to have someone else instruct us. Whenever he was around, she couldn't take her eyes off him and she totally ignored me. One day, as we rode the bus to a practice route, I bemoaned Hedy's lack of affection, telling the trainer, "When I requested a dog that wasn't obsequious, I had no idea what I was asking." Wryly her trainer replied, "Neither did we. We had to look it up."

Hedy had also adored Heather, her puppy raiser. Heather was a determined young woman, even at 16. For 18 months, she socialized Hedy, introducing her to sounds, different kinds of transportations, smells, and environments. She made sure Hedy was secure and felt safe no matter what unfamiliar thing came her way. In the mornings, Hedy would somersault out of her crate into Heather's lap, put her two front legs on Heather's arms, and give her a "Hedy hug."

The instructor was an Alpha person, but I was the second daughter of a Confucian scholar in a family of Alphas. I learned early that I was not to even think of being an Alpha. So I didn't. And when I was in guide dog school, having to be the Alpha of the team so my dog would respect and bond to me, I didn't know how.

Being blind doesn't automatically mean they give you a dog. You must show yourself competent to handle a strong, intelligent sentient being. To earn the right to take Hedy home, I had to exhibit a profound change of demeanor, one that was sufficiently Alpha-esque to convince Hedy that I meant what I said. Since I was strict and consistent after we got home, she came to trust me enough to guide reasonably well. But she didn't love me. And, to tell the truth, I didn't love her either. It's hard to love someone who doesn't want to be close.

I talked to Heather about it. It wasn't that Hedy couldn't love; she was crazy about Heather and her trainer. She just didn't love me. It broke my heart. But maybe that was the issue. She had loved intensely and completely two other significant people, and now she had been torn away yet again. I was person number three. Maybe it wasn't safe to give her heart to yet another person who might disappear from her life.

As it turned out, that was the case. Over the years, she would choose to give me a bit of her heart—one piece at a time. By the end, we were so bonded that we couldn't bear to be separated. We were truly one entity—a unit so united that our very identities were bound together. But that would take years. This poem celebrates the first of those incremental gifts of heart, like the black stallion on the desert isle, learning to trust Alec Ramsey by the blue lagoon.

SPRING HAPPENING WITH HEDY
on the fifteenth week with Hedy

She watches me now.
And sometimes lies close.
On her own.

They said this would happen.
I thought it would not.
She's too stubborn:
I'm too strained.

But I don't get to be
the only one
not lovable enough—
exception to the tried and true
sixty-some years of proof:
You do the work.
You take your place—steady at the helm.
You be the Source.
Insist.
Persist.
Correct-reward-and praise.

It happens
like little buds pushing
dark bare sticks
to blossom
It happens
like lilies
from cold dumb globes
spearing through spring soft soil
gallantly green and white.
It happens
like leaves.
It happens
because
it happens.

It happens
because I want to
want her to
want to
so much

And she does
now
because
she does
like blossoms
like lilies
like leaves

Leash Relieve

We were taught to relieve our guide four times a day, and always on leash. Why? Because it's important to know what is going on inside your guide. You can tell a lot about her health from what comes out of her and how often.

Before Hedy, I had decades of writing books—spending all day working at my computer. After Hedy, I had to go out four times a day, at very specific intervals, and make sure she "did her business."

It was an interruption. I wasn't happy. Also, I wanted her to get to it and be done with it so I could get back to work. But she didn't. She had to contemplate, evaluate, savor.

Relationships interrupt your life. They're inconvenient. But in the midst of adjusting to and accommodating the needs of a new being, you might find a whole new reality beyond the narrow confines of what you've established for yourself, and you might see things that for years you've been missing.

LEASH RELIEVE

Every day
four times a day
every early morning
to night after dark
I take you
out.

You
sniff the morning
sniff the evening
sniff the noon
and afternoon
stare down the distance
where scent of deer has passed.

Ten minutes they say
but you're not even trying—
you're greeting the morning
regarding it
a new delicacy
offered promise of
pleasures yet untasted.

Four months
I have watched you
four times a day
savor the air
in all its complexities
overtones
and meanings.

I take you out
so you can
Do Your Business.
I tell you
it's for you
but
I stand

feeling evening on my skin
and sometimes
even
see
a star

THE NOBILITY AND EQUALITY OF COMMON PURPOSE
a political and social observation

Plastic bags are needed now.
Large or small, they're treasures now.
Clear, opaque or in-between—
Valued, all, in my esteem.
White or blue, red, yellow, black,
Safeway, K-Mart, Nordstrom Rack,
Produce, bread bag, merchandise,
Not too thin is really nice.
Twice a day they do their work
Picking poop up off the dirt
Showing in all matters fecal
plastic bags are proven equal

I went to guide dog school two years after my husband Dennis had his strokes. At first I tried to take care of him at home as my father had done for my mother. Daddy told me he had taken vows when they got married, and he inteneded to keep them. For seven years he tended her, and I watched the King of the Castle become the loving partner my mother had always wished he would be.

Many relationships were healed during those seven years, especially among my parents and me. We became a team helping one another in the times of deepest vulnerability all the way to the end. It was terrible and beautiful and most magnificent. I wanted that for Dennis and me, but there were stairs, there was Sundowner's, and I couldn't see well enough to clean up after him. After more than a year of struggles, I finally admitted he was too much for me or my son John, who had taken him to his house, saying Dennis had been a good step-father and he wanted to do this for him. Broken-hearted, I settled my husband in a care facility. I felt I'd failed him.

As Dennis' dementia progressed, he required increasingly attentive levels of care. Kimberly, who had taken care of Dennis' father and mother, now took on the responsibility for her father, moving him to a memory care facility near her. It was three hours away from me.

My young friend Nathan was not adverse to long drives and had, in fact, driven me as often as he could, the 500 miles so I could help my father take care of my mother in her terrible illness. One day I felt the Lord nudge me to visit Dennis. Nathan was available, and we arrived on the day the Lord had specified.

When I walked in, Dennis was asleep. I figured I'd wake him by stroking his arm and singing some of my songs to him. His eyes opened, filled with fury. I stepped back just in time to avoid a blow as he took a swing at me. "Why are you singing my wife's songs?" he yelled.

Shocked I fled the room, weeping as I hurried down the hall towards the door. I was bewildered. Is that what the Lord wanted me to see—my husband so sunk into dementia that he didn't recognize his wife of nearly thirty years?

A beloved caregiver waylaid me in the hall and talked me into going back. I didn't want to, but she was insistent. Dennis was asleep when she spoke to him quietly. "Mr. Greenlee," she said gently, "your wife is here."

Heavily, Dennis opened his eyes. "My wife?" he asked. Then, looking at me, he said with a little smile, "Hello, Kid." It was his fondest term for me, my favorite one. For a few moments he was back, the man I had married. For a few minutes, he remembered me, and I remembered him.

Not long after, Kimberly called. The facility had informed her that she would have to find somewhere else for her father to live. He had sent another caregiver to the hospital and his violence was increasing. She had finally found a place that would take him, but she needed me to come and tell him. I made arrangements immediately to be there the next day, October 27.

The night of October 26, I sat on the floor watching "The Black Stallion," the movie I watched when I needed something to soothe my mind. I get engulfed in the stunning images of the ebony Arabian, too wild for any human. Yet Alec Ramsey becomes his trusted friend. There's a scene when the boy and the horse are playing in the lagoon, the underwater view of the strong black legs against the beautiful blue, the thin legs of the boy close by, then on the back of the stallion, then galloping joyously on the beach in a bond no one else may share.

I always wanted a bond like that—one where the other would love me above all others, an extraordinary connection into which no one else is invited. I had hoped it would be with Hedy, but, though she now chose to be in the same room with me, she still stayed several yards away.

I tend to sit on the floor when I'm disturbed. I don't know why. Maybe it's about getting lower. Anyway, that night, as I sat on the floor watching the movie. Hedy came over, and snuffing, pressed against me, somersaulting into my lap, then lying next to me, still touching.

Early the next morning, the phone rang. It was Kimberly. Her dad was gone. It was 4:55, she said, and it made me think of Dennis' favorite song, number 255 in the hymnal—"I'll Fly Away." A couple of years before, he had asked me, "Why doesn't Jesus take me home?" Now he had his heart's desire. In the cool early hours of October 27, on his father's birthday, Dennis had flown away, straight to the arms of Jesus, Whom he had so wanted to see.

Nathan drove me the long way to say my final good-bye. I was too stunned to talk. You expect it. You know it's inevitable. You even know it will be better—for everyone. But you're still shocked. Death is like that—shocking. It was never meant to be. That night, I sat on the floor of my bedroom, staring at the blue carpet, too numb to think or sleep. Hedy came, putting her front legs on my arms, giving me a Hedy hug. In her brown eyes, I saw compassion I had never seen, a connection beyond all others that only we could share.

Connection

Nearly two years
I've waited
looking in your
small brown canine eyes—
do you see me
as more than
the food lady
who takes you
good-smelling places
where you don't get to eat?

I kept it strict:
no pet, no talk, no play,
no interaction of any kind
except with me
so I would be your everything
and you'd want only me
Black stallion on the desert isle

You do your job.
In the long run,
isn't that enough?
It has to be.
I said yes to you
for better
or at least
for good.

But Monday night
as I sat trying to
settle my soul with
the gorgeous wild horse,
elegant ebony
grand piano legs
churning blue lagoon
following the boy
snuffing to fill
his huge heavy head

with more of
whom he loved,
you came
snuffing,
rubbing your face in my lap,
butt up,
churning upside-down,
still snuffing,
then plopping,
still touching...

Did you know?
Did you know it would be tomorrow,
the call before dawn
when it can't be good?
When you sniffed the bed and
wagged your tail
didn't you know
he wasn't really there?

Do you know what it means to die?
Do you understand beyond the
vacancy of chair
comprehend within
the wracking
wordless wait
as friends empty the room
honoring the airless
unspeakable
twist of
fundamental
universal
nothing unnatural
consequence of birth
while I try to ignore the
outrageous
unreal disconnect
from what has been for better
and worst
and worse

but in the blue of our own room
night of drizzle and no stars
no more thick cable of worry
stretching unbearably three hours north,
you come
sit before me
looking up
I kneel
You put your
black as grand piano legs
on my arms
small round canine eyes
brown
and sad
as mine

THE TRUTH OF RAINSOAKED PINE MESS

I thought I'd cry without stopping, sobbing for months till I was so dehydrated there could be no tears left. But I didn't. I was shocked, stunned to silence and no coherent thoughts. My father was gone. He had told me it would be soon, showing me the bulge in his belly where the aneurism was growing visibly almost every day. My husband had died exactly two weeks before, and the overlapping griefs were overwhelming.

Perhaps this poem will give you a sense of that strange, restless place where the long-dreaded phone calls have come and everyone you've worried about for decades of tending is gone. It's a peculiar disconnect, but the reality of today, like pine litter sticking to your shoes, is undeniably real and must be faced. You must acknowledge the truth, and you cannot run away.

THE TRUTH OF RAINSOAKED PINE MESS

This morning I went out
Rain had pounded parts of pine
to the ground redbrown limp
and everywhere
I was walking
thinking
plan the service pick the music
write the life
slivering it into
words charged by the column inch

For years I've thought
always elsewhere
bracing for the next ill wind
now
walking the dog
I hear multiple callings
of vees flying south
my mother's only
truly happy memory
and I'm past
and I'm thinking next week
but underfoot the redbrown litter lies
sticking to my shoes
tracking in my house
truth of today
unrelenting:
I'm pounded to the ground
with no way to fly south.

Reconfiguration with Wings

This poem is easier to understand if you're familiar with the process that takes place between caterpillar and butterfly. It's not a make-over, thick stumps lengthening into slender articulated legs, eyes that can barely discern dark and light becoming compound with 180 degrees of sight and discernment of color far more acute than ours. Metamorphosis. It's not a do-over; it's a complete transformation. For that to happen, extreme measures must occur. Inside the chrysalis, the caterpillar turns to soup. A few discs remain, migrating to where they will become eyes, wings, internal organs. They contain the instructions, the blueprint and order for what's to come. And they're called, wonderfully enough, "Imaginal Cells."

RECONFIGURING WITH WINGS
Three Days After My Father's Death

They say you're always a child in your father's house.
Will I become a grown-up now?
Fast melt within the chrysalis of pain

You don't see it, I suppose,
eyes gone runny with all the rest—
Not till after
when you've fought free
struggled from the transparent shell
do you understand
it took all that
for this
to begin

I started writing books to keep my family line in the historical record. At the time, there wasn't much available on the Chinese-American experience, only a few things on railroad workers. Neither of my parents' parents were railway workers. So I wrote the stories of my parents' childhoods, and then began books on their life together.

But there was illness and crisis after crisis and, by the time I was ready to write the astonishing story of what had opened before the feet of these two children from difficult pasts, they were gone. *Eternal River - The Next Thirty Years,* had to be written without them, and it was hard. I couldn't ask them questions. I couldn't check facts or the dates of inventions. And I didn't know what to leave out. Of course, there's no one left to dispute what I wrote, but I wanted it to be true in every sense, representing with clarity and grace that extraordinary time when they were in their prime, life was golden, and the future was full of light.

WRITING A BOOK

after finishing "Eternal River, Volume III,
The Next Thirty Years"

Writing a book is not as hard
as digging a ditch
or fighting a war.
but writing a book
can take your eyes
steal your sleep
pillage your past
Writing a book
can keep alive
things that were
that might have been
forgotten

Writing a book requires time
the sacrifice
of what is now
Writing a book
means sitting inside
hands on the keys
eyes on the screen
while evening breeze
speaks sweets unrepeated
but time
requires
writing a book

Writing a book
can keep alive
things that were
that might have been
forgotten
things that ought not be
forgotten
or
remembered

Some things of mine
ought not be forgotten
though they're harder than dirt
or fighting a war
things worth
the digging
the fighting
the grind of
past eclipsing
sweet-smelling evening
for some things of mine
ought not be forgotten
and there's no other way
save
writing a book
harder than dirt
or fighting a war

FOR THOSE WHO HAVE GONE BEFORE

I saw you last night,
all of you—all of you talking and
walking
though you couldn't
I'm certain
you
couldn't
I thought you were dead.
said
Aren't you dead?
How could you be
here
and me so near
as if years
have no holes
where you used to be

Perhaps
as they say
it's not what I thought —
not a stop
but a pause
nothing more
nothing less
not a sob
but a breath
just a breath
just a
breath
or a sweet
soft
sigh

www.ingramcontent.com/pod-product-compliance
Lightning Source LLC
Chambersburg PA
CBHW071816020426
42331CB00007B/1499